Sacred Space in a Song and a Prayer

Raise Your Vibration and Sing from Your Soul

A D R I E N N E   G I L L

BALBOA
PRESS
A DIVISION OF HAY HOUSE

Balboa Press books may be ordered through booksellers or by contacting:

Balboa Press
A Division of Hay House
1663 Liberty Drive
Bloomington, IN 47403
www.balboapress.com
1 (877) 407-4847

Because of the dynamic nature of the Internet, any web addresses or
links contained in this book may have changed since publication and
may no longer be valid. The views expressed in this work are solely those
of the author and do not necessarily reflect the views of the publisher,
and the publisher hereby disclaims any responsibility for them.

The author of this book does not dispense medical advice or prescribe the use
of any technique as a form of treatment for physical, emotional, or medical
problems without the advice of a physician, either directly or indirectly. The
intent of the author is only to offer information of a general nature to help you
in your quest for emotional and spiritual well-being. In the event you use any
of the information in this book for yourself, which is your constitutional right,
the author and the publisher assume no responsibility for your actions.

Any people depicted in stock imagery provided by Thinkstock are models,
and such images are being used for illustrative purposes only.
Certain stock imagery © Thinkstock.

Printed in the United States of America.

ISBN: 978-1-4525-1529-8 (sc)
ISBN: 978-1-4525-1530-4 (e)

Balboa Press rev. date: 10/1/2014

Dedication

This book is an acknowledgement of the songs and prayers given to me by Grace. I dedicate each word, every lyric to the healing and the joy that they bring to you, to me, to everybody, and I am eternally grateful to Thee.

Contents

Introduction in song

I love me unconditionally
Take my hand come sing with me
I love me unconditionally
God loves me
I am one with Thee

Song 1

I'm Letting Go Now

When I was young they told me
You've got to live in the dark
Stay out in the cold

When I was young they told me
You better run and hide
Or they'll swallow you whole

When I was young they told me
You've got to marry the guilt girl
And live with the shame

When I was young they told me
You've got to carry your cross
And suffer in pain

Well I'm letting go now and I'm free
I see the light now, I see it clearly
I'm not afraid now to be me
I'm letting go, and I'm free

Now in time I'm older
I sing and I play
And love in the moment

Now in time I'm bolder
I dance in the sun
Now my life has begun

I'm letting go now and I'm free
I see the light now, I see it clearly
I'm not afraid now to be me
I'm letting go and I'm free

Ya who are they anyway?
I just erased them all
Who are they anyway?
I put the sun back in my day
Who are they anyway?
I shine a light over them

Cause I let go, and I'm free
I see the light, I see it clearly
I'm not afraid to be me
I let go, and I'm free

Free, ya I'm free
I see the light now, I see it clearly
I'm not afraid now, to be me
Ya I'm free, ya I'm free
I'm not afraid now to be me
To be me, to be me
I'm letting go and I'm free!!!

Prayer 1

I Am Light

I am light
I am love
I am everlasting beauty
I am eternal youth
I am holistically healthy
I am unconditionally happy
I am forever free
I love me unconditionally
Now through eternity

Song 2

Miracles

You've got to believe in miracles
Look around you, they surround you
Open your eyes, your heart, your mind
And they come from the sweet Divine
Yes they come from the sweet Divine! <3

Prayer 2

Happy and Free

Happy, happy, happy and free
That's me

Playing, saying and singing
Sweet melodies

Happy, happy, happy and free
That's me

Living, laughing and serving God
With glee

Happy, happy, happy and free
That is surely me!

Song 3

I Am Joy

I am joy
I am love
A precious gift from above
And I know it
And I feel it in my soul

Prayer 3

I Choose Love

I choose to align with love today

And everyday

I choose to get out of my own way

And make way for love! <3

Song 4

Rise Above the Pain

Rise above the pain
Listen to your inner voice
We're all one in the same

Rise above the pain
Rise above the pain

We're all here to seek the truth
We're all one and in the same

Rise above the pain
Rise above the pain

Have no fear there is no shame
Rise above the pain

Rise above the pain
Rise above the pain

Listen to your inner voice
We're all one and in the same

Rise above the pain
Rise above the pain

We're all here to seek the truth
We're all one and in the same
Have no fear there is no shame

Rise above the pain
Rise above the pain
Rise above the pain

Mmmm mmmm
Mmmm mmmm
Mmmm mmmm

Prayer 4

Trust

I trust you Dear God
I am patient I am listening
I have clear vision
I am open to receiving all the goodness
And abundance in the Universe!

And so it is!

Song 5

Forgiveness

You say forgiveness will set me free
You say forgiveness turn the other cheek
You say forgiveness just follow me
I'll be here forgiving me

Forgiving me yayay
Forgiving me yayay

Well I'll just be here forgiving me

Prayer 5

Acceptance

I have learned
When I separate myself from all that is
I suffer
I now accept all that is
Including me
I now see beauty in everyone and
everything
Especially in me
I am thankful to Thee

Song 6

It's All About Love

It's all about love
Hugs and kisses
It's all about love
Don't you miss it?
It's all about love
That's why we're here
It's all about love
And I love you dear!

Prayer 6

Language of Love

I am open to giving and receiving love
Love is my native tongue
I speak it fluently and most frequently
This pleases me and sets me free

Song 7

I am One With The Universe

I am one I am one with the Universe
So are you so are you
Yes it's true
I am one I am one with the Universe
You feel it in everything you do
I am one I am one with the Universe
Yes it's true yes it's true
So are you
I am one I am one with the Universe
I feel it in everything you do

Prayer 7

Poems of Three

I

It's easy to be me
It's easy to be free
Why would I want to be
Anyone but me?

II

Accepting me for me
Is quite easy for me
I am free to just be

III

I am me
You are me
We are one
With Thee
I now see

Song 8

To Just Be

Wondering and waiting for which way
    things are gonna go
Cautiously anticipating is it you are
    you gonna show?
Playing the movies in my mind am I
    gonna shine
Releasing the pain and now I know
    that it's time

I finally decided to be free
I finally decided just to be
I finally decided which way
    I'm gonna go
And it's easy, it's so easy to just be

Remembering how to breathe letting
    in that gentle breeze
Going with the flow and letting go....
Alive and awake to say it's a brand
    new day
And loving me is the game that I'm
    gonna play

I finally decided to be free
I finally decided just to be
I finally decided which way I'm gonna go
And it's easy, it's so easy to just be

The past is over and forgetting who I am
Those days are gone forever
Now I know now I understand

Cause I finally decided to be free
I finally decided just to be
I finally decided which way I'm gonna go
And it's easy, Lord it's so easy, to just be,
    it's so easy

To just be
To just be
To just be...........

Prayer 8

Goodness

I accept all as goodness

It is all the same

It is all love

Situations vary and choices wane

I now release the doubt, the sorrow,
the shame

Because I know now it's all goodness
it's all the same

Song 9

Love Is the Answer

Love is the answer
Love is the key
Love unlocks the door to heaven
Love sets you free

Love love love
Love love love
Love love love love

Open your eyes
Feel your inner truth
Live life in the moment
Do what you do with

Love love love
Love love love
Love love love love

I'm talking about love love love
love love love
love love love love

Prayer 9

A Call To Divine Mother

I call upon your beauty and strength

Lift my spirits higher than the heavens

Divine Mother sweet complete nurturance

Embrace me with your everlasting tenderness

Song 10

My Beautiful Baby Girl

You are my sunshine my beautiful
   baby girl
You are my sunshine
And I'll love you till the end of time
You are my beautiful baby girl
You are my sunshine
And I'll love you till the end of time
My beautiful baby girl

Prayer 10

I Love You Princess, I Love You Handsome

Stories and lullabies
Butterfly kisses
Swinging and swaying
Sea shell beaches
Hugs and tickles
Goodnight kisses
I love you princess
I love you handsome
Dreams come true
Brightest wishes

Song 11

My Baby Boy

You bring me love
You bring me joy
I thank god above you're my baby boy

Your heart is full of light
Pure as gold
I thank God above you're my baby boy

Prayer 11

Just breathe

How familiar to me
The beauty the grace and ease
That it is to just be me
Ahh , just breathe

Song 12

Feel It

Feel it, feel it
Raise your vibration
Heal it, heal it
Cause we are worth it and we are perfect
Feel it, feel it
Raise your vibration
And feel it, and heal it
Cause we are worth it, and we are perfect
Feel it, feel it, feel it, feel it...

Prayer 12

Shine

Now is the time
Now I rise and shine
Every glorious day in every vibrant way
Sweet innocent sunshine
Now is the time

Song 13

The Miracle I've Been Waiting For

I'm looking in the mirror
Checking out my make-up
And I caught the sparkle from the
    corner of my eye

And I got this feeling this feeling I've
    been waiting for
And I got this feeling, this is the
    miracle that I've been waiting for
And I got this feeling, and I'm so
    grateful for it

Now you're a big part of my life
And everything's coming up roses
And I pledge my heart to you until the
    end of time

Cause I got this feeling this feeling I've
    been waiting for
And I got this feeling, this is the
    miracle that I've been waiting for
And I got this feeling, and I'm so
    grateful for it

Yes I wrote it in my journal
Talked to God and all the angels
Opened up my heart to all the love and
    all the strangeness

And I got this feeling this feeling I've
    been waiting for
And got this feeling, this is the miracle
    that I've been waiting for
And I got this feeling, and I'm so
    grateful for it

And I got this feeling, this feeling,, and
    I'm so grateful for it

I got this feeling

Prayer 13

Transformation

It came up and in my face
The deepest darkest painful place
I looked at it square in face
I sent it love and a warm embrace
Now this place has transformed into
        beauty and Grace

Song 14

It's the Journey

It's the journey
It's the journey
Now I see it's all meant to be

It's the journey
It's the journey
And I love it and I love me
I love me, I love me

Now I'm home now I know
It's the journey it's the journey
And I love me, I love me

Sacred Space in a Song and a Prayer

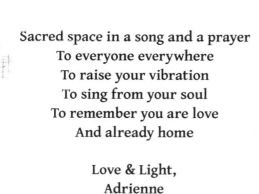

Sacred space in a song and a prayer
To everyone everywhere
To raise your vibration
To sing from your soul
To remember you are love
And already home

Love & Light,
Adrienne

Adrienne Gill is a holistic healthcare practitioner, a Massachusettes licensed massage therapist and certified polarity practitioner (energy worker).

Opening up to and accepting Grace's gifts of poetry and song Adrienne has discovered the healing power of unconditional love and creative expression in Sacred Space in a Song and a Prayer, may it contribute to the healing and raised vibration of everyone everywhere.